OUR
GRE★T
STATES

WHAT'S GREAT ABOUT
INDIANA?

✳ Candice Ransom

LERNER PUBLICATIONS ✳ MINNEAPOLIS

CONTENTS

INDIANA
WELCOMES YOU! ✱ 4

Content Consultant: Jason Lantzer, Instructor,
Butler University

Lerner Publications Company
A division of Lerner Publishing Group, Inc.
241 First Avenue North
Minneapolis, MN 55401 USA

For reading levels and more information, look
up this title at www.lernerbooks.com.

Main body text set in ITC Franklin Gothic Std
Book Condensed 12/15.
Typeface provided by Adobe Systems.

Library of Congress Cataloging-in-Publication
Data

Ransom, Candice F., 1952–
       What's great about Indiana? / by
Candice Ransom.
          pages   cm. — (Our great states)
       Includes index.
       ISBN 978-1-4677-3871-2 (lib. bdg. :
alk. paper)
          ISBN 978-1-4677-6273-1 (eBook)
       1. Indiana—Juvenile literature. I. Title.
F526.3.R36 2015
977.2—dc23   2014020487

Manufactured in the United States of America
1 – PC – 12/31/14

INDIANA Welcomes You!

The Crossroads of America is a great motto for the state of Indiana. It has many highways that lead to exciting places. You can explore the wonders of Indiana. Maybe you'll crawl through a cave. You might listen to the loud engines at the Indianapolis Motor Speedway. Try camping under the stars; canoeing on lakes; or enjoying a tall, cold glass of fresh milk at a dairy farm. Check out the world's largest children's museum too! Read on to learn about the top ten things that make Indiana great! You just may stay awhile.

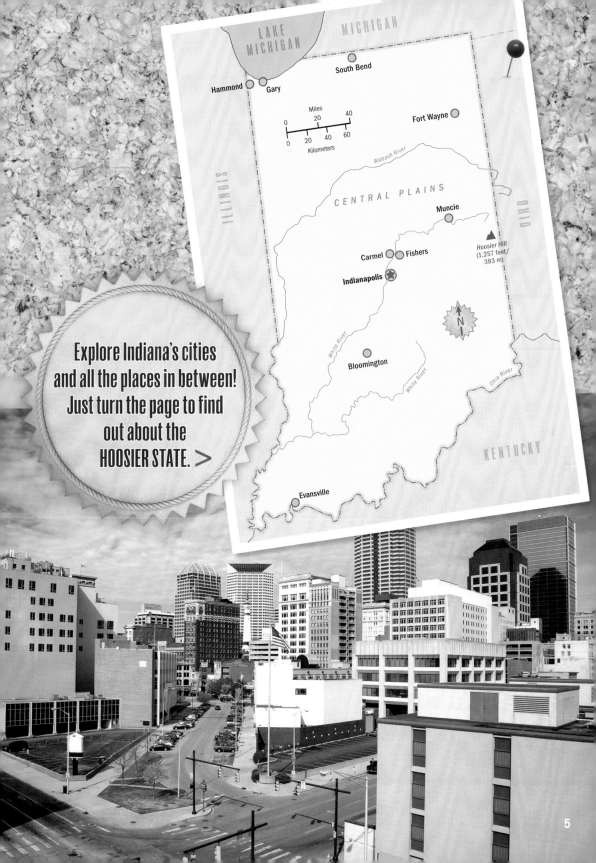

LAKE
MICHIGAN

MICHIGAN

South Bend

Hammond Gary

Miles
0   20   40

0   20   40   60
Kilometers

Fort Wayne

Wabash River

C E N T R A L   P L A I N S

Muncie

Hoosier Hill
(1,257 feet/
383 m)

Carmel Fishers

Indianapolis

N

White River

Bloomington

White River

Ohio River

KENTUCKY

ILLINOIS

OHIO

Evansville

Explore Indiana's cities
and all the places in between!
Just turn the page to find
out about the
HOOSIER STATE. >

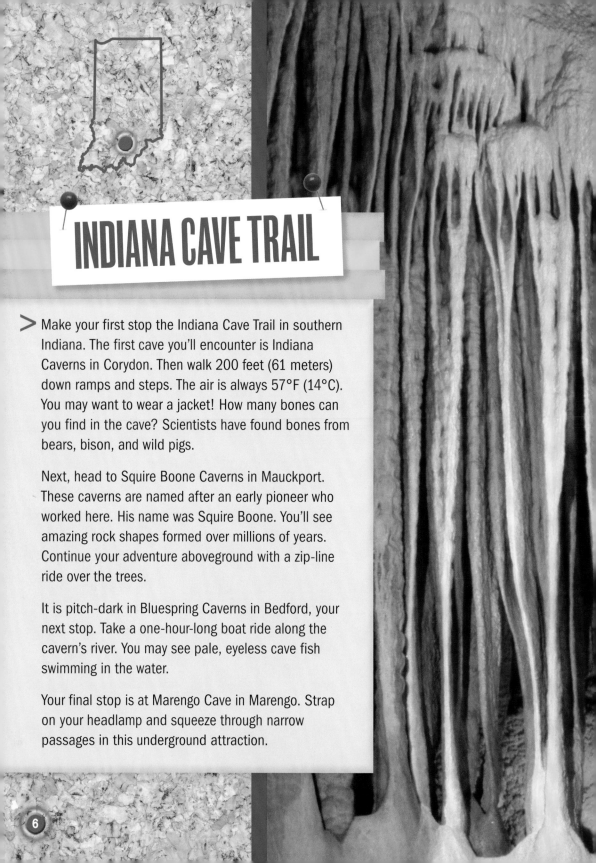

INDIANA CAVE TRAIL

> Make your first stop the Indiana Cave Trail in southern Indiana. The first cave you'll encounter is Indiana Caverns in Corydon. Then walk 200 feet (61 meters) down ramps and steps. The air is always 57°F (14°C). You may want to wear a jacket! How many bones can you find in the cave? Scientists have found bones from bears, bison, and wild pigs.

Next, head to Squire Boone Caverns in Mauckport. These caverns are named after an early pioneer who worked here. His name was Squire Boone. You'll see amazing rock shapes formed over millions of years. Continue your adventure aboveground with a zip-line ride over the trees.

It is pitch-dark in Bluespring Caverns in Bedford, your next stop. Take a one-hour-long boat ride along the cavern's river. You may see pale, eyeless cave fish swimming in the water.

Your final stop is at Marengo Cave in Marengo. Strap on your headlamp and squeeze through narrow passages in this underground attraction.

All the caves on the Indiana Cave Trail feature bats hanging from the ceiling! These creatures are fascinating and harmless to people.

CAVERNS AND CAVES

A cave is a natural underground hole. A cavern is a system of caves connected by passages. Indiana's caves were formed from glaciers that once covered most of the state. Rushing water from the melting glaciers hollowed out many caves and caverns in southern Indiana's soft limestone bedrock.

INDIANAPOLIS MOTOR SPEEDWAY

> You'll know you've arrived at your next stop when you hear the loud roar of car engines. The Indianapolis Motor Speedway has been a popular spot among locals and tourists since 1909. Here you can watch professional drivers speed around the 2.5-mile (4-kilometer) racetrack.

The Speedway hosts the famous Indianapolis 500 race in May every year. Grab a seat in the world's largest stadium. Then cheer loudly for your favorite driver! After the race, take a ride with a professional driver in an IndyCar. You'll go much slower than the typical race speed of 215 miles (346 km) per hour.

You won't want to miss the Indianapolis Motor Speedway Hall of Fame Museum. Check out the Marmon Wasp. This car won the first Indianapolis 500 in 1911. Make sure to look at the other seventy-four cars on display too.

You'll see cars and the Indianapolis 500 trophy on display at the Indianapolis Motor Speedway Hall of Fame Museum.

CONNER PRAIRIE

INTERACTIVE HISTORY PARK

> Indiana's history comes to life at Conner Prairie Interactive History Park in Fishers. Explore exhibits from pioneer days to the Civil War (1861–1865).

Stop in Prairietown, a historic community set in 1836. Meet the townspeople and take a lesson at the schoolhouse. You may want to dress up in pioneer-style clothing. Or try out a children's game.

If you visit in March through November, stop at Lenape Indian Camp. Walk through a typical American Indian home. You can also hop into a handmade canoe and pretend to paddle down the river.

Next, save Indiana from Civil War raids. In 1863, Confederate general John Morgan and his men rode into southern Indiana. They burned bridges, ripped up railroad tracks, and stole horses. Park workers dress up as soldiers. Help them fight back by carrying the US flag into battle. Or gather medical supplies for wounded soldiers.

Visit the schoolroom, *left*, or the general store, *right*, at Conner Prairie Interactive History Park.

INDIANA STATE FAIR

> Nothing represents Indiana like the State Fair! The first fair was held in 1852 to support the state's farming. Located in Indianapolis, the modern state fair has a lot more than corn and hogs. Exhibits, contests, rides, food, and shows will keep you busy for a week!

Visit the Glass Barn and see how the food you eat goes from farm to grocery store. You'll hear a lot of mooing, bleating, and crowing as you wander through the livestock exhibits. Pedal your own toy tractor in the youth tractor pull. Dip your fishing pole in the Fishin' Pond to try to catch a catfish.

The midway is the place for rides, food, and games. Try the Silver Streak, Mega Drop, Yoyo, and Screamer rides. Race down the Fun Slide on burlap sacks. Then test your pitching skills at Skee-Ball.

After all the fun, you'll probably be hungry. You'll find favorite snacks like pizza and hot dogs. Or you may want to try something new such as bacon doughnuts or deep-fried candy bars.

DAIRY FARMING IN INDIANA

Many settlers brought a cow with them when they came to Indiana. Starting in the 1850s, dairy farms provided milk for local stores and households. Indiana is one of the fastest-growing dairy states in the United States. It ranks fourteenth in the nation in dairy cattle and is home to more than sixteen hundred dairy farms.

Hot dogs, cotton candy, and deep-fried candy bars are just a few foods you'll find at the Indiana State Fair.

You can see North America's largest water clock at the Children's Museum of Indianapolis.

CHILDREN'S MUSEUM OF INDIANAPOLIS

> Dinosaurs peek in the window! More dinosaurs break out of a wall! This could happen only at the Children's Museum of Indianapolis.

Watch stars spin in the SpaceQuest Planetarium. Your next stop is the Treasures of the Earth exhibit. Figure out who is buried in an Egyptian tomb. Learn about the pirate captain William Kidd. Climb around a pile of cannons. You can even try on scuba diving gear. See real Spanish coins, cannonballs, and old bottles from other shipwrecks.

There's more! Climb a rock wall or build a parachute. Imagine being the engineer on the Reuben Wells. Built in 1868, this 55-ton (50-metric-ton) steam train was the most powerful in the world at the time.

The Dinosphere takes you back 65 million years. Hear dinosaurs roar as the sky changes from day to night. Full-size skeletons stand among plants.

Touch a Tyrannosaurus rex bone and dig for fossils in the Dinosphere exhibit.

FORT WAYNE CHILDREN'S ZOO

> Do you want to see animals from around the world on your trip to Indiana? You can at the Fort Wayne Children's Zoo! Start your visit at the Central Zoo area. Watch sea lions leap from the water for a fish. This training helps them exercise. Hear that shriek? That's a peacock. You'll see them wandering around loose. Take a train ride past the Indiana Family Farm.

At the Australian Adventure exhibit, watch sharks and deadly jellyfish in the aquarium. After you leave the aquarium, be on the lookout for bats, parrots, and other flying animals. Enjoy a canoe ride down the river.

Next, walk through the Indonesian Rain Forest area. Paths lead you through the jungle to the endangered orangutans. Farther down the trail, you may even see endangered tigers.

Your last stop is the African Journey trail. This trail lets you see zebras, hyenas, and lions. Let giraffes eat lettuce from your hand on the giraffe platform. Take a photo in an explorer's tent.

You'll see peacocks wandering loose at the Fort Wayne Children's Zoo.

Kangaroos hop around the Australian Adventure exhibit.

17

ANGEL MOUNDS
STATE HISTORIC SITE

If you visit Indiana in the fall, take a hayride at Angel Mounds State Historic Site.

> Travel back to ancient times at the Angel Mounds State Historic Site in Evansville. This 603-acre (244-hectare) wildlife preserve has eleven grass-covered mounds. Mississippian American Indians built the mounds between 1000 and 1450 CE. Scientists believe the mounds served as platforms for huts. Climb the wooden steps to the top of the central mound. A chief may have lived here many years ago.

During the Native American Days festival, you can become part of the village. Watch people perform traditional American Indian dances. Grind corn for a meal, and play games American Indians used to play at the site. Kids worked hard back then. Even their games taught them skills, such as hunting or cooking.

Try your skill at archery. Ride your bike on trails that wind through the woods. Or get lost in a spider-shaped corn maze!

MISSISSIPPIAN INDIANS

The name *Mississippian American Indians* came from the Mississippi River valley. Many groups of American Indians came from that area and spread to other regions. They spoke different languages but shared a way of life. These people lived in large villages along rivers. They hunted game and fished. They also grew corn, beans, squash, sunflowers, bamboo cane, and tobacco.

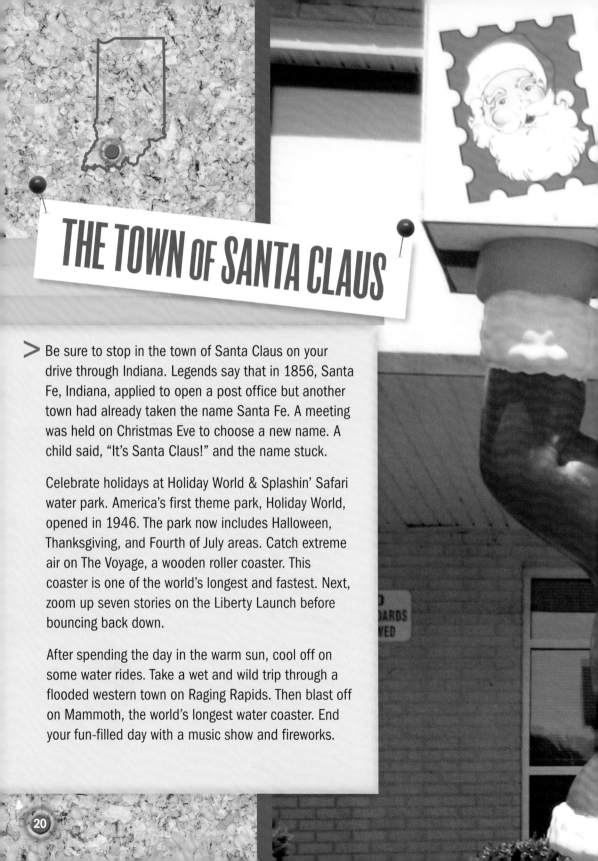

THE TOWN OF SANTA CLAUS

> Be sure to stop in the town of Santa Claus on your drive through Indiana. Legends say that in 1856, Santa Fe, Indiana, applied to open a post office but another town had already taken the name Santa Fe. A meeting was held on Christmas Eve to choose a new name. A child said, "It's Santa Claus!" and the name stuck.

Celebrate holidays at Holiday World & Splashin' Safari water park. America's first theme park, Holiday World, opened in 1946. The park now includes Halloween, Thanksgiving, and Fourth of July areas. Catch extreme air on The Voyage, a wooden roller coaster. This coaster is one of the world's longest and fastest. Next, zoom up seven stories on the Liberty Launch before bouncing back down.

After spending the day in the warm sun, cool off on some water rides. Take a wet and wild trip through a flooded western town on Raging Rapids. Then blast off on Mammoth, the world's longest water coaster. End your fun-filled day with a music show and fireworks.

ITED STATES POST OFFICE

Santa Claus, Indiana

47579

Statues of Santa Claus can be found all across the town of Santa Claus.

LINCOLN BOYHOOD
NATIONAL MEMORIAL

> Step back in time at the Lincoln Boyhood National
Memorial in Lincoln City. Abraham Lincoln, the
sixteenth US president, grew up in Indiana. Learn more
about Lincoln at this park.

Start your visit at the visitor center. Watch a short
movie on Lincoln's life in Indiana. Stand next to a
life-size cutout of Lincoln. He was 6 feet 4 inches
(2 m) tall. Then slip your feet into a replica of Lincoln's
shoes. He wore a size 14!

Walk from the visitor center to the Lincoln family's
cabin. Only the fireplace and outline of the cabin are
still there. The cabin was not very big. Next, head
over to the Living Historical Farm. You might be asked
to pick fresh green beans from the garden or wash
wool from a sheep. Or you could help shape wooden
handles for hammers.

Costumed park rangers at the Lincoln Boyhood Memorial perform chores that were done every day in the 1800s.

ABRAHAM LINCOLN

Abraham Lincoln lived in Indiana from the age of seven to twenty-one. He attended school for only a few years. The rest of the time he worked on the family farm. He chopped down trees and built fences. He loved to read books. This way of life taught Lincoln to be strong and responsible.

INDIANA DUNES

> End your Indiana trip with a visit to the beach! Lake Michigan has 15 miles (24 km) of shoreline in northern Indiana. Lake Michigan is the sixth-largest freshwater lake in the world.

Stop at the Indiana Dunes National Lakeshore to begin your outdoor fun. The dunes make this area famous. Strong winds off Lake Michigan cause sand to form tall ridges. Walk down 250 stairs in West Beach to the sandy shore. Put those strong winds to use! Go paragliding or fly a kite.

There is more to the Indiana Dunes than beaches and the lake. Ride your bike along the Calumet Dunes Trail. Keep your eyes open for snakes such as the little brown snake or the hognose snake. You can hike to the Pinhook Bog. Insect-eating plants such as the pitcher plant grow here.

Go swimming at nearby Indiana Dunes State Park. Pitch your tent at the park campground. Sleep under the stars and dream of coming back to Indiana.

Be on the lookout for blue racer snakes on the Calumet Dunes Trail.

You can hike through a bog at the Indiana Dunes National Lakeshore.

YOUR TOP TEN!

You've read about ten fun things to see and do in Indiana. Now it's your turn! What would your Indiana top ten list include? Grab a sheet of paper and make your own Indiana top ten list. What would be your favorite places to visit? What would you do there? Then turn your list into a book. Illustrate it with your own drawings or pictures from the Internet.

INDIANA BY MAP

> MAP KEY

⬟ Capital city

◯ City

◯ Point of interest

▲ Highest elevation

–·–·– State border

▬▬ Indiana Cave Trail

Visit www.lerneresource.com to learn more about the state flag of Indiana.

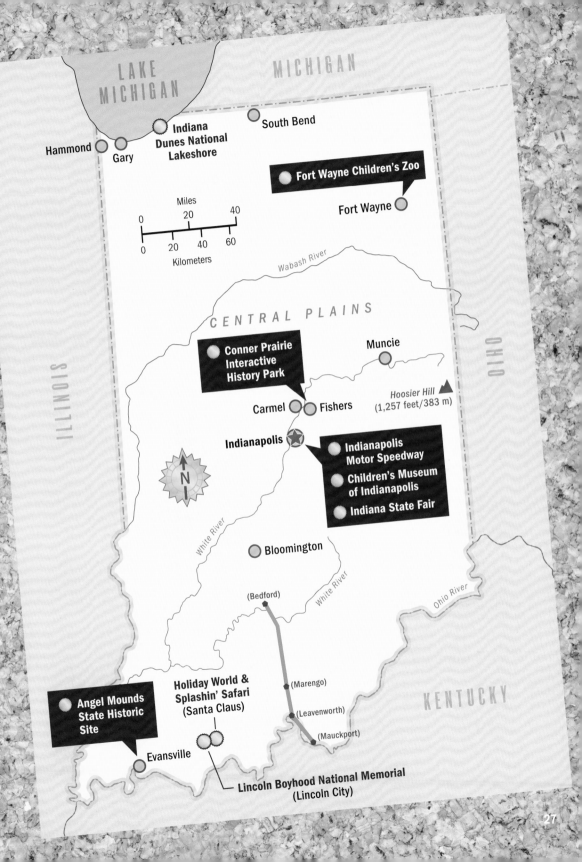

LAKE MICHIGAN

MICHIGAN

Hammond

Gary

Indiana Dunes National Lakeshore

South Bend

Fort Wayne Children's Zoo

Fort Wayne

Miles
0   20   40
0   20   40   60
Kilometers

Wabash River

CENTRAL PLAINS

Conner Prairie Interactive History Park

Muncie

Hoosier Hill
(1,257 feet/383 m)

Carmel   Fishers

Indianapolis

Indianapolis Motor Speedway

Children's Museum of Indianapolis

Indiana State Fair

N

White River

Bloomington

(Bedford)

White River

Ohio River

Angel Mounds State Historic Site

Holiday World & Splashin' Safari
(Santa Claus)

(Marengo)

(Leavenworth)

KENTUCKY

(Mauckport)

Evansville

Lincoln Boyhood National Memorial
(Lincoln City)

ILLINOIS

OHIO

INDIANA FACTS

NICKNAME: Hoosier State

SONG: "On the Banks of the Wabash, Far Away" by Paul Dresser

MOTTO: "The Crossroads of America"

> **FLOWER:** peony

TREE: tulip poplar

> **BIRD:** northern cardinal

DATE AND RANK OF STATEHOOD: December 11, 1816; the 19th state

> **CAPITAL:** Indianapolis

AREA: 36,184 square miles (93,716 sq. km)

AVERAGE JANUARY TEMPERATURE: 28°F (–2°C)

AVERAGE JULY TEMPERATURE: 75°F (24°C)

POPULATION AND RANK: 6,570,902; 16th (2013)

MAJOR CITIES AND POPULATION: Indianapolis (834,852), Fort Wayne (254,555), Evansville (120,235), South Bend (100,800), Hammond (79,686)

NUMBER OF US CONGRESS MEMBERS: 9 representatives, 2 senators

NUMBER OF ELECTORAL VOTES: 11

NATURAL RESOURCES: gas, oil, coal, limestone, sandstone, shale, gypsum, peat

> **AGRICULTURAL PRODUCTS:** beef, cattle, corn, eggs, hogs, milk, soybeans, turkeys

MANUFACTURED GOODS: chemicals, processed food and beverages, transportation equipment

STATE HOLIDAYS AND CELEBRATIONS: Lincoln's Birthday

GLOSSARY

bedrock: solid rock lying under soil

bog: wet, poorly drained ground

Confederate: a word to describe a soldier or citizen of the Confederate States of America

dune: a hill or ridge of sand piled up by the wind

endangered: threatened with extinction

exhibit: an object or collection of objects on display

glacier: a large body of ice and snow that moves slowly over land

limestone: a rock formed from shells or coral

paragliding: a sport where a person jumps from a high place and uses a special parachute to float to the ground

professional: a person who does an activity as a job

Expand learning beyond the printed book. Download free, complementary educational resources for this book from our website, www.lerneresource.com.

FURTHER INFORMATION

Braun, Eric. *John Green: Star Author, Vlogbrother, and Nerdfighter*. Minneapolis: Lerner Publications, 2015. Read about a famous resident of Indiana—John Green, author of the best-selling book *The Fault in Our Stars*.

Explore the States: Indiana
http://www.americaslibrary.gov/es/in/es_in_subj.html
Read informative stories about Indiana at this site.

Figley, Marty Rhodes. *President Lincoln, Willie Kettles, and the Telegraph Machine*. Minneapolis: Millbrook Press, 2011. This thrilling tale from the Civil War will put readers right in the action.

Indiana: Facts, Map, and State Symbols
http://www.enchantedlearning.com/usa/states/indiana
Learn more about Indiana's symbols, plus try some fun activities.

The Indianapolis Public Library Kids' Blog
http://www.imcpl.org/kids/blog/?page_id=12286
Look at photos, get ideas for projects, and learn about famous Hoosiers.

Piehl, Janet. *Formula One Race Cars on the Move*. Minneapolis: Lerner Publications, 2011. Learn more about some of the cars that race at Indianapolis Motor Speedway.

INDEX

PHOTO ACKNOWLEDGMENTS

The images in this book are used with the permission of: © Kenneth Keifer /Shutterstock Images, p. 1; NASA, pp. 2–3; © Katherine Welles/Shutterstock Images, p. 4; © Todd Taulman/Shutterstock Images, pp. 4–5; © Laura Westlund/Independent Picture Service, pp. 5, 27; © Layne Kennedy /Corbis, pp. 6–7; © Ethan Daniels /Shutterstock Images, p. 7 (top); © Iphoto /Shutterstock Images, p. 7 (bottom); © carroteater/Shutterstock Images, p. 8; © ciapix/Shutterstock Images, pp. 8–9; © Michael Snell/Alamy, p. 9; © Tom Uhlenbrock/MCT/Newscom, pp. 10–11; © Peter Ptschelinzew/Alamy, p. 11; © Alexey Stiop/Shutterstock Images, pp. 12–13; © Gary L. Brewer/Shutterstock Images, p. 13 (bottom); © Marcl Schauer/Shutterstock Images, p. 13 (top); © David R. Frazier Photolibrary, Inc./Alamy, p. 14; © National Geographic/SuperStock, pp. 14–15; © Micha Fleuren/Shutterstock Images, p. 15; © Samuel Hoffman/The Journal-Gazette/AP Images, pp. 16–17; © rickyd/Shutterstock Images, p. 17 (top); © idiz/Shutterstock Images, p. 17 (bottom); © Jason Clark/The Evansville Courier & Press/AP Images, pp. 18–19; © Gvictoria/Shutterstock Images, p. 18; National Park Service, pp. 19 (bottom), 22–23, 23 (top); © Kevin Pang /MCT/Newscom, pp. 20–21; © Franck Fotos /Alamy, p. 21 (top); Library of Congress, p. 23 (bottom); © Delmas Lehman/ Shutterstock Images, pp. 24–25; © Psychotic Nature/Shutterstock Images, p. 25 (left); © Jacek Jasinski/Shutterstock Images, p. 25 (right); © nicoolay/iStockphoto, p. 26; © Fragolini/Shutterstock Images, p. 29 (top right); © Birds and Dragons/Shutterstock Images, p. 29 (top left); © Jonathan Lenz /Shutterstock Images, p. 29 (bottom right); © Sea Wave/Shutterstock Images, p. 29 (bottom left).

Cover: © EPA European Pressphoto Agency b.v. / Alamy (cars); © iStockphoto.com /tacojim (dunes); © Don Klumpp/Getty Images (Children's Museum); © Laura Westlund/Independent Picture Service (map); © iStockphoto.com/fpm (seal); © iStockphoto.com/vicm (pushpins); © iStockphoto.com/benz190 (corkboard).